Chorley
Past

CHORLEY
Guardian

at heart ♡ publications

First Published in 2007 by:
At Heart Ltd, 32 Stamford Street, Altrincham,
Cheshire, WA14 1EY.

in conjunction with

The Chorley Guardian,
32a Market Street
Chorley
PR7 2RY

To Dad —
" Happy Birthday "
2009.

All ow Pone
fone - xxo.
o x
x .

ISBN: 978 1 84547 136 1
Printed by Bell & Bain, Scotland.

Contents

Foreword

WHEN I joined the *Chorley Guardian* as Editor in April 2006 I could never have fully appreciated then how much the experience would have changed and enriched my life.

The paper was established in 1871 and now has readers from all over the world.

I know this is true because of all the emails and letters I get from ex-pats.

What shines through in the correspondences is that you can take the man out of Chorley but you can't take the Chorley out of the man!

Many of the emails I get are requests for copies of a former *Chorley Guardian* book that we produced called *'Images of Chorley'*. It was published in 1994 when Steve McLean was the paper's Editor.

I'm sad to report that Steve is no longer with us. He died of cancer five years ago while we both worked at the *Bristol Evening Post* but I consider myself fortunate to call him a friend. I had no idea that I would eventually follow in his footsteps in coming to Chorley but I share his passion and enthusiasm for the town and its residents.

Like Steve 13 years ago, I'd also like to put on record my thanks to the late, great former *Guardian* Editor George Birtill. Many of the photos in this book were taken by him. Although the captions may have changed to reflect the way the town has changed there's no mistaking the clarity of the pictures and the images they convey of another era. My thanks also go to his son David for his help in producing this book and two well known Chorley historians, Jack Smith and Barry Lowe, in checking the captions.

Finally I would like to thank the paper's Assistant Editor Vanessa Taylor, who is a truer Chorlean as it's possible to find. Her knowledge of Chorley is matched only by her genuine affection for the town and it shines through in the book.

The various images in the book try and capture the changing face of Chorley and the people that help shape the town's past. Some of the pictures have almost iconic status. Others capture simple scenes from the workplace or the sports fields.

The book has been produced in conjunction with At Heart Publications and we hope you get as much enjoyment from reading it the book as we have in selecting the photos contained within.

Most of us enjoy nostalgia and we hope this book will bring back many memories for readers of the life and times of people in Chorley, and the places, some of which have changed beyond all recognition over the years. We hope you like your own personal trip down memory lane.

Chris Maguire
Editor
Chorley Guardian
November 2007

Out and About

■ Procession to celebrate the Coronation of King Edward VII in 1902. The Big Lamp was on the left, as is the Market Street Sunday School.

■ Preston Street, Chorley, in a time where everybody knew, or was related to, everybody else, and as soon as the photographer erected his tripod, people came from nowhere.

■ This image was taken during the First World War, showing a soldier pushing his bicycle, in the foreground of the photograph, along Birkacre Brow. Riversdale is on the right, and Birkacre Cottages, now demolished, on the left.

■ Children playing outside on the deserted Birkacre Brow, taken in 1934, from the entrance to the Bleachworks. Riverside House on the left is where the mill engineer lived. Birkacre Cottage, and Sunnymount are on the right.

■ A lone cyclist pedals away from St. George's Church around 1910. St. George's Church was designed by the famous architect, Thomas Rickman, who also designed St. Peter's, Preston and Blackburn Cathedral. The church was built by a 'Mr Rich' of Wigan who ironically went into bankruptcy afterwards.

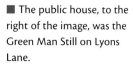 Before Church Brow became steps. In Hollinshead Street on the right are the two houses which were converted into a pub, called the Swann With Two Knecks. The sign outside the church shows that the congregation were in the process of raising £6,000 for a new church organ.

■ The public house, to the right of the image, was the Green Man Still on Lyons Lane.

■ There were several mills based along Lyons Lane, the one featured on the right of our 1958 image, was one of the oldest.

■ This row of houses, near Lyons Lane railway bridge, was nick-named 'Piss-pot' row, having been built when 'petties' or loos were shared with your neighbours in joined backyards. The urine was collected by a local mill which added it to mill water; the process gave strength to the cotton fabrics once they had been soaked. A urine collection 'tub' is on display at Helmshore mill.

■ The Borough allowed Ribble to lease land near the 'Flat Iron' for their first Bus Station, shown in the picture. The present Bus Station has an enlarged site. Southbound buses left from this side of the 'island' station. Northbound buses left from the other side.

■ Shovelling snow in this winter scene outside the Red Lion Tap, Bank Mount.

■ J.W. Stone's grocery shop, on Market Street, was a popular meeting place and shop for local people. The owner, Mr Stone, was a prominent member of Chorley's Council. Next door to Stone's was The Red Lion, an old coaching house, that was replaced by The White Hart.

■ Long since demolished these former handloom weavers cottages were built on Botany Brow.

■ Massive changes were taking place in this 1934 photograph, as Botany Bridge was being widened, under the guidance of contractor, Leonard Fairclough. The steam crane seemed to be attracting interest from passers-by.

■ A bigger bridge at Botany was built by Fairclough's to span the M61.

■ Devonshire Road was numbered from Pall Mall end, because it was mainly a footpath through fields, before the St. Thomas's Road end was opened in 1920. It was asphalted in the mid 1960s so that traffic noise would not interfere with St. Mary's School and Church, pictured right. Since this photograph was taken, the school has moved to Hornchurch Road and Sumner's corn mill, the tall building on the right was demolished and the site used for offices.

■ Chorley's famous Big Lamp was situated at the top of Market Street, at the junction with Pall Mall and Bolton Road. The much-loved lamp was a popular meeting place.

■ Crowds pack Market Place at the turn of the century. Note the cart loads of goods parked between the shops and stalls.

■ Group of children photographed on the Preston Road, Whittle-le-Woods.

■ Children gather before one of the most popular attractions – an organ grinder and live monkey. The 'Unter Den Linden' café in the background advertised its chipped potatoes, fried fish, Scotch scones and suppers. The photo was taken on the corner of New Market Street with Chapel Street.

■ Fazakerley Street was once a popular extension of Market Street. Above Hilton's shoe shop was the Kingston Café, popular with American GIs during World War Two. View of Fazakerley Street from Market Street.

■ This picture of the covered stalls is taken from New Market Street looking towards Fazakerley Street and the Town Hall.

■ Chorley Town Hall, seen from Park Road early 1900s. Note the buildings on the immediate left in front of St. Laurence Church at the Market Street end of Union Street.

■ Chorley Town Hall pictured in 1946.

■ A public meeting outside the Town Hall announcing election results, possibly in the 1940s.

■ The old Chorley Town Hall jutting out on the right, Craven's grocers (once the Police Station) and the Royal Oak, pictured in 1936.

■ The Chorley Town Hall Christmas Tree in 1955.

■ Chapel Street, Chorley. St. Mary's Church towers in the background but there is no arch in this picture. Note the statue of Disraeli, a supporter of the Primrose League.

■ Chapel Street, always the popular shopping street in Chorley. Various buildings were demolished, like the arcade on the left. Further on, Haydock's timber yards and sawmill are very obvious. This picture was taken from St. Mary's tower in September 1955.

■ Steeley Lane in the 1960s.

■ Market Street, pictured around the 1920s.

■ A view of the then cobbled Market Street, believed to be around the turn of the century. Note the horse-drawn coal cart in the left foreground.

■ Market Street in the late 1950s. The Bulge, as it was known, on the right of the street, later disappeared as Market Street was widened.

■ The double kerb at the top end of the Market Street in the 1950s shows how the pavement has been raised.

■ Market Street Bulge: Christie's snack bar, on the right, started what was known as the Bulge. Four Shops in a row extended outwards from the line of the remaining shops. The buildings, which were declared unsafe, were demolished to widen the road.

■ Not only was traffic hindered by a narrow Market Street but old buildings set too far forward obscured the ancient Parish Church, as this picture of the entrance to Union Street and Church Brow clearly shows.

■ New Market Street had its traffic problems even when the Victoria Hotel was on the corner with Chapel Street.

■ The junction of St. Thomas's Road and Dole Lane – the buildings are now gone.

■ Union Street was the busiest two-way street in the town centre. It links Market Street with the new town centre by-pass and the traffic is so heavy at times that the Bus Station has been relocated elsewhere. This picture was taken in the late 1960s.

■ The old Royal Oak Hotel, Market Street, was an institutional part of the town. An old coaching house, it recalled past grandeur. Chorley folk were angry at the proposal to demolish it in 1936, but apart from other considerations, the road was too narrow and the Government was calling for implementation of the town centre improvement scheme.

■ Cheapside in 1972. The shop on the far left of the picture is now San Marco's Restaurant and St. George's Church can be seen in the background of the image.

■ Bagganley Hall in 1966 – it was demolished to make way for the M61.

At Work in Chorley

■ Before the turn of the century, Chorley had its own version of Woolworth's at the corner of Fazakerley Street and Market Street. The Lyon's shop used the more famous store's policy of selling nothing for more than sixpence.

■ Crowds used every vantage point possible to watch passing parades especially walking days, including the old offices of the Chorley Guardian and Leons Tailors in Market Street.

■ The original newspaper shop at Higher Wheelton, situated on Blackburn Road. Standing in the doorway on the right is Mr Edward Tomlinson, the owner of the shop.

■ New Market Street has always been important to shoppers. Seen here as it was in the 1970s, all buildings on the right have been demolished as part of the town centre re-development, which began in 1994.

■ The Prince Albert in Market Street, between Halliwell Street and Anderton Street, in 1870. The landlord in the doorway is Thomas Gillett. He had ten sons who formed a band to entertain the clientele.

■ Parsons' charabanc outside Yates's Wine Lodge. Mr Parsons started at Leyland Motors in Chorley, then began his own bus and charabanc service. Charabancs appeared to wait in West Street in the front of Yates's, as in this picture. The charabanc was a Vulcan model.

■ The Woodlands Hostel, Southport Road. During World War Two it housed workers who came to build the ROF as did Highways Hostel Euxton and afterwards accommodated foreign workers from various countries. When the new police station was built, the administrative offices were housed in the office buildings.

■ Buckshaw Farm, Euxton, unseen by the public for many years because it used to lie in the middle of the restricted Royal Ordnance Factory grounds and now it is in Buckshaw Village and due to undergo renovation. This photograph was probably taken around 1910.

■ By the 1960s there is little evidence of the former cattle market here. During the war, the only sales were from stalls provided by the auctioneer. On this picture the cattle pen site is occupied by the gas showroom which has since been demolished to make way for Market Walk. The café on the left began when the Royal Ordnance factory was built – Irish labourers liked food when they had a drink or two and it was known as the Bus-bar. This has also since been demolished

■ Decimalisation arrives in Chorley. From 1971, all market prices were shown in old pence and new currency.

■ "Farewell Miss" – Mrs M.Salmon, assistant mistress at Weldbank St. Gregory's RC School, receives a writing case from pupil Maureen Baxendale to mark her retirement after 40 years of teaching in the town. Left to right: Miss Calderbank, Mrs Kirkham, Mrs Salmon, Miss Grayken, Miss Lucas, Maureen Baxendale and headmaster Mr P.Turner.

■ Princess Margaret toured St. Michael's School in October 1975. Also seen here is the domestic science teacher, Miss Fisher.

■ The Old Technical School, Chorley. The building is still used as the Town Library and County Council Education Offices.

■ Clara Fairhurst at work, weaving in Rice's Mill in 1920.

■ A Coronation scene at Rice's Mill for King George VI in 1937.

■ Birtwistle's Mill, Abbey Village, spinning room in 1910. They lady on the right is Annie Nightingale.

■ Rice's weavers dressed up for the Coronation of George VI in 1937.

■ Birtwistle's Mill, Abbey Village. Eight ladies
pictured in the weaving shed in 1910.

■ Working on the Jacquard
looms in 1957.

■ Working on the spinning frame at the Talbot Cotton Mill, Chorley, in the 1950s.

■ In stitches – Charlie Drake, seated, Michael Medwin, Norman Rossington and Fred Mawdesley with workers at the Chortex Mill.

■ Celebrity visit – comedian and actor Bob Monkhouse with Lawrence Cooper, right, at E.H.Cooper's Chortex Mill weaving shed, October 1957.

■ Star visit: actors Fred Mawdesley, Norman Rossington, Michael Medwin and Charlie Drake visit the warping room of E.H. Cooper's Chortex Mill in the late 1950s.

■ Group of bleaching girls and boys who worked in the croft, possibly in Birkacre, near Coppull, in the making-up room. The picture is from the 1920s.

■ A group of tambouring girls at Birkacre. In the middle at the back is Mrs Morris, who trained the tambourers – workers who embroidered cotton products.

■ Two shire horses from Birkacre won prizes at the Preston Royal Show in the 1920s. Mr Caunce, on the right, prepared the horses, and his helper John Yates is on left.

■ A steam wagon taking pitmen home from Birkacre Colliery. The speed was limited to 12mph, or 5mph with a trailer attached.

■ A group of bleaching girls, sitting on a hill in Birkacre. Some of the girls, especially on the front row, look no more than ten years old.

■ Rebuilt after a fire, this massive factory was still known as a Heapey Bleachworks when serving a different purpose. In the end it was Thomas Witter's. The site has now been redeveloped as a housing estate.

■ Swansey Mill at the time of the 1953 Coronation of Queen Elizabeth II.

■ Witters product being taken to the goods yard by horse.

■ Six men outside a refreshment hut, taken on Moor Road, Chorley. They may have been either miners, because of the tough clogs and watches, or mill workers.

■ Empty shell stores at the ROF during World War Two.

■ Filling anti-tank MkII mines during World War Two at the ROF.

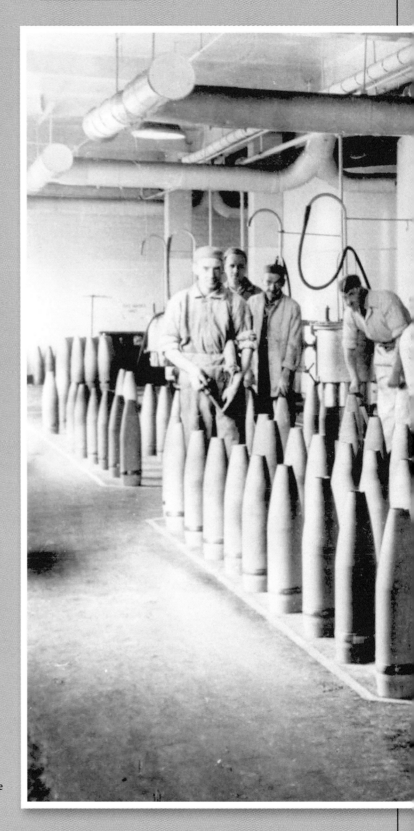

■ Filling six-inch howitzer shells at the ROF in wartime.

■ Coming off shift at Welch Whittle Colliery in January 1960.

■ The last shift at the closure of Ellerbeck Colliery near Coppull, in August 1965. The last man coming out of the cage was a Mr Richardson.

■ Farewell – miners gather to bid a happy retirement to Sam Biers, centre left, on his last day at Ellerbeck Colliery in 1961.

■ The last shift on, 31 March 1967, at Chisnall Hall Colliery near Coppull. This ended coal mining in an area that had been rich in 'black diamonds'.

■ The building of Chorley North Industrial Estate in the 1970s.

■ Chorley Gas Works pictured in July 1956. Situated in Chorley Bottoms this undertaking became famous. When a member of the council complained about a dreadful smell from Chorley Bottoms, he was referring to the undertaking which had belonged to the local authority from early days and was one reason why street lamps were lit by gas until after World War Two. Nationalisation removed this from Chorley's management, although two gasometers at the top of the hill are a landmark.

Transport and Emergency Services

■ Complaints about Chorley Railway Station were not confined to the crossing. The whole station looked untidy and shabby, particularly the 'Elephant Tanks' used for filling boilers on steam engines.

■ Chorley Goods Depot, has long since gone and is now replaced by the town centre by-pass road.

■ The old Chorley Station and crossing in 1970. Although the signal box man was supposed to let traffic through the level crossing, the busy line was not always safe for this.

■ Chorley Railway Station, showing the crossing gates. The footbridge was later replaced by the 'subway'.

■ Only seven of the nine railway arches landmark are visible from this point in Knowley Brow. They carried the Chorley to Blackburn line until it closed. The Nine Arches were finally demolished in 1969 to make way for the M61 motorway.

■ Funeral carriages, outside Greatorex Livery Stables, by this time petrol was the motive power.

■ A group outing in a wagonette – a familiar sight in Chorley around the turn of the century. The identity of the passengers and date of the picture are unknown.

■ Parsons' charabanc outside the Wheatsheaf in Coppull, 1914, taking a party on an outing.

■ Buses on the 'Flat Iron'. Before the first Bus Station was built in 1927, buses collected on the side near the Cattle Market.

■ Chorley town centre has changed beyond recognition over the years – and this photo proves it. Thought to have been taken in the 1950s/60s it shows the junction of Chapel Street and Market Street. On the corner is Stringfellows florists, which has since moved to the market. It also shows a car apparently about to turn the wrong way into a one way street.

■ The petrol-driven bus belonged to the Lancashire and Yorkshire Railway Company and was a link between Chorley, Whittle-le-Woods and Bamber Bridge.

■ The Dallas family firm ran buses through Wheelton village until they were bought by Ribble. The bus ran every half hour to the Conservative Club at Withnell and twice on Saturdays. Mr Les Smith (right) opened the Clock Garage in Wheelton in 1946.

■ The new bus route worked, but Chapel Street, once one-way up, became one-way down. It is now pedestrianised.

■ 'Four Skamps' taxi drivers at Chorley Station, 1920. The taxi firm was called Bannisters.

■ On 30 October 1969, to mark the M61's opening, crowds were allowed to walk the length.

■ Prime Minister Harold MacMillan opens the Preston stretch of the M6 in 1958. 'Preston By-pass' as it was known became Britain's first motorway.

■ A royal day for the Anderton Services on the M61. The Queen and Environmental Secretary Peter Walker are seen leaving the opening of the services in October 1971.

■ Temporary traffic lights were installed at the Duke Street and Lyons Lane crossing. They were dispensed with only when the by-pass came through in 1994.

■ Schoolchildren learn about the process of law and justice in proper surroundings. It will be noted the furnishings, especially the dock with its spikes and bars, that this was the old Courtroom. While the new Courthouse was being built, justice was dispensed in the Lancastrian Room of the Town Hall. Solicitor front left centre was Tom Wallwork.

■ March 1963. Police dogs were a deterrent, especially during periods of trouble between youths from Chorley and neighbouring towns.

■ Chorley people were fond of the combined Police Station and Courthouse in St. Thomas's Square, but it was not nearly big enough for work that increased greatly after World War Two.

■ Rawcliffe Hospital, Gillibrand Street, Chorley, pre-1933 when the new hospital was built at Hartwood. After 1933 it became the Chorley Rural District Council Offices, then in 1974 (local Government reorganisation) it became Chorley Borough Planning Department. Now the home of Chorley Community Housing.

■ The official opening of Chorley and District Hospital in September 1933, 40 years after opening of the first Chorley Hospital. The opening ceremony was performed by the Earl of Crawford and Balcarres. The hospital had three wards – the Rawcliffe Ward for men, Winstanley Ward for women and the Samuel Ward for children. There was one operating theatre. Another one was added later.

■ Christmas in the Rawcliffe Ward at the New Chorley Hospital, 1935. Many mill owners gave money for the hospital and much was raised through charity events and donations. There was a 'Hospital Fund' for 1d a week, which entitled the member to free treatment.

■ Girls from St. Mary's choose the 1966 Hospital Queen at the first of the Chorley District Hospital Welfare Society's charity dances.

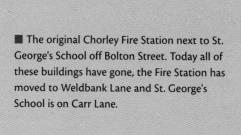

■ The original Chorley Fire Station next to St. George's School off Bolton Street. Today all of these buildings have gone, the Fire Station has moved to Weldbank Lane and St. George's School is on Carr Lane.

■ One of the first jobs tackled by the first Borough Council was to provide a fire-engine with a steam-powered pump. On 19 June 1884, everyone turned out in their Sunday best when it was christened 'Bobs' after Lord Roberts. But getting up steam proved a dirty business and the onlookers were covered with soot and dirt.

■ The local fire-brigade adjust the hands of the clock on Chorley Town Hall.

■ Proud and shining – a Chorley fire-engine crew in ceremonial uniform. The motorised engine was made by Leyland Motors.

Sport and Leisure

■ In 1932 a poll was held on the Sunday opening of cinemas in Chorley. It was successful, but did not save the cinemas. Television heralded the decline of many of them in the 1950s and 1960s. Those in the photograph were the managers of the six cinemas that Chorley once had: The Odeon, Plaza, Pavillion, Royal, Empire and former Hippodrome.

■ The Odeon Cinema, Market Street, note the poster for Sunday cinemas in Chorley. Today the building is being used as a Gala Bingo Hall.

■ England and Preston North End star Tom Finney, third from left, hands over prizes to the winners of a cine-camera competition at the Odeon Cinema in the 1950s.

■ Royal Theatre, Market Street, later became a cinema, then a supermarket, then hamburger restaurant, and is currently empty awaiting redevelopment.

■ An aerial set up to provide a TV broadcast from Chorley Town Hall.

■ A concert party called 'The Somebody's' from Water Street School, around the time of World War One.

■ The Adlington Music and Arts Society members in their production of *Maritza* at the Christ Church School in 1965.

■ Chorley Amateur Dramatic Society performers in the panto, *Dick Whittington* in February 1955, at The Little Theatre, Dole Lane.

■ The Man-Jan Dancing School entered as the cast of *The King and I* in the 1965 Adlington Carnival.

■ Tom Finney opens the new extension of Coppull British Legion Club in the 1950s.

■ This building served as Chorley Borough Library for more than 80 years. Demands increased to such an extent that it was agreed the County Library Service should take over. The former Chorley Grammar School and later Chorley College on Union Street, proved the ideal building and the County Library Service assumed control on the 12 June 1986. The old Library was demolished and a health centre built on the site.

■ Trinity Church Orchestra, well known in the locality. At the piano is Noel Sellars, a superb local organist. The occasion is probably the Sunday School anniversary with the assembled childrens', ladies' and gentlemen's choir.

■ The Railway Hotel, Steeley Lane, on the right of the picture, featured bowling tournaments, despite the fact the green was said to have been built over a mineshaft. Healds Iron Foundry can be seen on the left.

■ Bowlers at the Old St. Mary's RC Church Club.

■ St. Laurence's Church Lads' Brigade in 1930 on the Parish Church bowling green, Park Road. Leader Major Lofthouse is fourth from left, front row.

■ September 1957 – St. George's 'B' team, winners of the Chorley Churches Bowling League, receive their trophy from the Mayor of Chorley, Councillor T. Grime.

■ The former boating pond in Ashley Park.

■ The Men's Guild of St. Mary's RC at the church club swimming pool in 1906. The enterprising Guild members volunteered to dig the 51ft x 21ft pool for free. Each paid five shillings (25p) to inscribe their name on a brick. The water in the pool, which was heated, was changed each week. It was built as an alternative to club life and the Revd T.S. Clark gave up his vinery for a changing room. The pool closed in 1938 following the opening of a Corporation-owned baths.

■ The The opening of Chorley Baths in 1938. The Baths were demolished and a new pool was built as part of the All Seasons Leisure Centre on Water Street.

■ Chorley Swimming Club about 1940. The building was in Railway Street and was privately owned.

■ An Austin rally at the covered Market Place in 1957.

■ Alderman John Green (left) pictured in 1946 studying plans for the Royal Agricultural Show. He is with Borough engineer Mr W. Lowe in the Mayor's Parlour.

■ Crowds at a Chorley Fairground, possibly pre-1910.

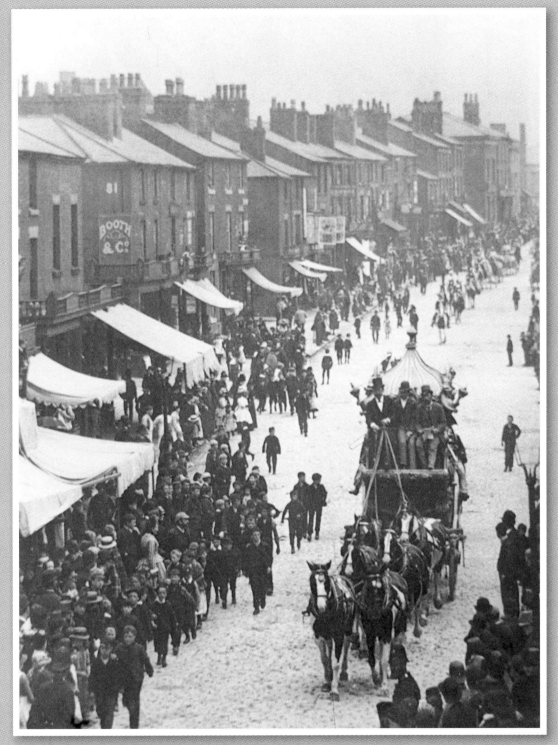

■ Another circus arrives in town, possibly just after the turn of the century. It is believed that the legendary Buffalo Bill – former Wild West Indian fighter William Cody – may have been the star attraction at this circus, seen arriving on Market Street.

■ The circus comes to town in May 1954 with elephants on parade in Market Street. Woolworths is now Argos.

■ Chorley's first bonfire night since the end of World War Two was held in November 1955. Explosives and other materials used in fireworks had been restricted until then.

■ 13 September 1957 – this big wheel provided a miniature Chorley illuminations, and was erected on the cattle market where another big wheel had been previously sited.

■ Coronation Street star Pat Phoenix who played Elsie Tanner, hands over a cheque on behalf of the Inskip League to County Councillor Tom Jackson at a dance held at Leyland Motor's Club in the late 1960s.

■ When Willie Lowe was Mayor in 1946-47, he realised an ambition to make full use of the Town Hall Assembly Rooms. His charity ball was a big success, and the Assembly Hall was christened. The Lancastrian entertainer Tessie O'Shea played her part too, making sure the right tickets go to the right prizes.

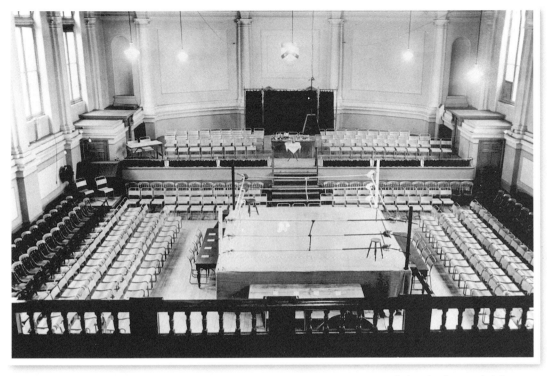

■ The Town Hall Assembly Room complete with balcony, with all arrangements made for Chorley Boys' Club boxing tournament. The balcony is now long gone.

■ Neighbours from Geoffrey Street, Chorley, going out for a day trip in a motorised wagonette in the 1920s. They usually went to visit the countryside. The wagonette was capable of 12mph, as marked on its side.

■ A happy group from St. Mary's RC Church prepare for a day trip abroad an Ogden's luxury coach in 1932.

■ July 1959. Chorley 'Wakes-week' holiday crowd takes an early holiday from the old station. A train also waits at the Blackburn platform, which was later dispensed with.

■ Staff at the famous Butty Bar – the Bus Station café – setting out on a day trip 30 years ago. The Butty Bar, another well-known Chorley institution, was closed down in July 1994 to make way for the town centre redevelopments.

■ A procession to mark the Coronation of King Edward VII in 1902.

■ A Chorley Walking Day before 1910 on Park Road with St. Laurence's Church seen in the background.

■ Chorley Walking Day of 1911. The father of the girl in the black hat had died that Easter. St. Laurence's group are seen here outside Booth's shop at the bottom of St. George's Street. The children had red, white and blue flowers that year to mark the Coronation of George V.

■ The Boys' Brigade on Coronation Recreation Ground. Probably taken on Walking Day. This is where they would assemble before walking around the parish boundary. Date unknown, believed to be 1930s.

■ Lawrence Road street party for the Coronation of Queen Elizabeth II in 1953.

■ The Chorley Guardian float in the town carnival of 1958. Standing by the driver's cab is then editor, George Birtill.

■ Singer Frankie Vaughan was a regular visitor to Lancashire and especially popular in Chorley. He didn't disappoint the excited crowd at Chorley Town Hall in August 1956, which is when this photo is thought to have been taken.

■ Children parade on horse-drawn wagons in what is thought to be the Rose Festival of 1925. The procession is seen in Bolton Street.

■ Hunters and horses find a popular calling place at the Black Horse at Limbrick, Chorley. Two members of the Holcombe Hunt await the rest of the hunt before chasing their quarry.

■ The hockey team at Chorley Grammar School, possibly 1934.

■ Adlington Cricket Club in 1904. Middle row, second from left, is Mr Middleton of Middleton's Mill.

■ Chorley Cricket Club team at Windsor Park, 1910.

■ Winners – Adlington Cricket Club won the Bolton and District Cricket Association Cup in 1914.

■ Members of Chorley CC and a Select XI line up before the benefit match for the dependents of the late Michael Norman. The game was played at Windsor Park on Sunday, 26 August 1965. Pictured left to right on the Chorley team: Jack Afflick (umpire), Doug Rossall, Martin Sherred, Oliver Demming, Albert Mockett (wk), John Mawdesley, Frank Henry, Bob Yardley, Eric Bateman, Alec Atherton, John Rossall (capt). Select XI (on the right) from the left: Gordon Edmundson (Blackpool & Leyland), Alan Bolton (Darwen & Lancs), Jim Bolton (Darwen, wk), Terry Ashcroft (Leyland Motors), Dave Sherrington (Chorley), Geoff Eccles (Darwen), Roy Booth (Blackpool), Peter Haydock (Darwen), David Higham (Preston), Dennis Porter (Leyland Motors), Ted Kelly (Chorley & Lancs) and Jimmy Halliwell (umpire).

■ Hut at Park Road tennis courts. On the right side was the ladies' changing room, on the left the men's changing room. In the middle was a refreshment bar. The picture was taken just after World War One.

■ A group of ladies on the tennis courts at Park Road in the 1920s. Anyone could play tennis there, although the courts were owned by Park Road Methodist Church.

■ Adlington White Star football team. John Slater MP is third from the left on the back row. The photograph was taken on White Star Field on The Common in 1904.

■ Mining side: The Ellerbeck Dundee football team from Ellerbeck coal mine, near Coppull, in 1908.

■ Football team on St. Laurence's Park 1909. The land belonged to St. Laurence's Park committee and was used as open space. The chimney in the background is a destructor chimney in Highfield Road.

■ Mighty Magpies – Chorley FC in 1957. Harry McShane, formerly of Manchester United, is pictured front right. His son, Ian, once a Chorley FC mascot, later went on to become an international film actor and star of TV's Lovejoy.

■ On November 2, 1957, around 8,000 fans turned up to see Chorley get beaten 2-1 by local rivals Wigan Athletic in an FA Cup match. Pictured here leaping in the air to send a towering header goalwards is Jack Cross. Cross was a no-nonsense footballer signed by Chorley from Lostock Hall as a centre forward but ended up playing as a centre half.

■ Chorley Football Club moved to their current home at Victory Park in the 1920s and consistently attracted big crowds. One of the best players was a local lad called Harry Davis, who played for the Magpies between 1913/14 and 1923, when he was snapped up by Port Vale. He's pictured here going in for a challenge with the goalkeeper in one of the first games Chorley played at Victory Park, although it's not clear who the opposition is. Watching the action on the right hand side of the picture is team-mate T. Price.